The Prime Minister is Ten Today

David Harmer was born in 1952. He lives in Doncaster with his wife Paula and his daughters Lizzie and Harriet plus five cats, four lizards, three fish and Blossom the puppy. David has been writing stories and poems for children and adults for many years. When he isn't doing that he is a primary school headteacher. He has appeared several times on radio and television and performs in the popular poetry duo Spill the Beans with his friend Paul Cookson. If David was in charge of the world these would be his laws:

1) No wars, famine, bullies, bad breath or homework.

2) Free chocolate for all.

3) Sheffield United to win every major competition, including the World Cup.

4) Did I mention the free chocolate?

5) Headteachers banned from wearing joke ties with cartoons on. Who are they kidding? The same goes for socks, by the way.

6) Four-day weekends.

7) Free entry for all children to every theme park in the world.

8) I am really, really serious about the chocolate.

Sam Hearn is the newly appointed Minister for Illustration. At the time of publication his exact whereabouts were unknown, although he can usually be found in his Party chair, between his Rt Hon. friends the Editorial Minister and the Minister of Design. Thank you and Goodnight.

Other books by Macmillan

WHEN THE TEACHER ISN'T LOOKING
Poems chosen by David Harmer

THE VERY BEST OF DAVID HARMER
Poems by David Harmer

THE TEACHER'S REVENGE
Poems chosen by Brian Moses

YOU'RE NOT GOING OUT LIKE THAT!
Poems chosen by Paul Cookson

TAKING MY HUMAN FOR A WALK
Poems chosen by Roger Stevens

MY STEPDAD IS AN ALIEN
Poems chosen by David Harmer

The Prime Minister is Ten Today

Poems Chosen by
DAVID HARMER

Illustrated by Sam Hearn

MACMILLAN CHILDREN'S BOOKS

For Paula, Lizzie and Harriet.

First published 2003
by Macmillan Children's Books
a division of Macmillan Publishers Limited
20 New Wharf Road, London N1 9RR
Basingstoke and Oxford
www.panmacmillan.com

Associated companies throughout the world

ISBN 0 330 41522 0

3 5 7 9 8 6 4

A CIP catalogue record for this book is available from the British Library.

Printed by Mackays of Chatham plc, Chatham, Kent.

Contents

When I am Prime Minister

When I am Prime Minister
The President Controller
Head Top Priority Number One Big Boss Chief
Manager of Everything
Answerable to No one
Totally and Utterly in Charge
Decision-Maker Supreme
I'm going to have my own office
And a sign on the door that says . . .

Prime Minister
The President Controller
Head Top Priority Number One
Big Boss Chief
Manager of Everything
Answerable to No one Totally and Utterly in Charge
Decision-Maker Supreme.

I'm probably going to need to get a bigger sign.
And a bigger door.

Paul Cookson

The Prime Minister is Ten Today

This morning I abolished
homework, detention and dinner ladies.
I outlawed lumpy custard, school mashed spuds
and handwriting lessons.
From now on playtimes must last two hours
unless it rains, in which case we all go home
except the teachers who must do extra PE
outside in the downpour.

Whispering behind your hand in class
must happen each morning between ten and twelve,
and each child need only do
ten minutes' work in one school hour.

I've passed a No Grumpy Teacher law
so one bad word or dismal frown
from Mr Spite or Miss Hatchetface
will get them each a month's stretch
sharpening pencils and marking books
inside the gaol of their choice.

All head teachers are forbidden
from wearing soft-soled shoes,
instead they must wear wooden clogs
so you can hear them coming.
They are also banned from shouting
or spoiling our assembly by pointing
at the ones who never listen.
Finally, the schools must shut
for at least half the year
and if the weather's really sunny
the teachers have to take us all
          to the seaside for the day.

If you're got some good ideas
for other laws about the
          grown-ups
          drop me a line in Downing
          Street,
     I'll always be glad to listen.
Come on, help me change a
          thing or two
before we all grow up
          and get boring.

David Harmer

More News from Downing Street

This afternoon we passed the following laws
On behalf of the children's party
Parents are not allowed to force-feed their children;
cabbage, sprouts, carrots
turnips, swede, and any other disgusting vegetables.

Parents are forbidden from using the following; because
I said so, in a minute, we'll see, wait till your father gets
home.

Parents are banned from buying and forcing you to
wear practical clothes you'll grow into eventually and
sensible out-of-date shoes.

It is now a criminal offence for Grandma or any other
aged female relative: to knit a jumper, or a cardigan, or
swimming trunks or a long Dr Who scarf as birthday
or Christmas presents, especially if you're thirteen with
a jumper with Thomas The Tank Engine on the front.

Bedrooms are parent-free zones at all times, as is the
bathroom first thing in the morning and all evening
and the same goes for the den behind the garden shed.

Evening curfews do not exist and bedtime is when we say.

Every child has the constitutional freedom to watch as
much television as they want, when they want, on
what channel they want, as loudly as they want, for as
long as they want.

The family CD player is now communal property.
Parents are forbidden to:
Like our music
Play their Beatles and Rolling Stones CDs
Dance at family parties
Dance with each other at family parties.

Mums and dads are prohibited from holding your
hand and kissing you in public in front of your mates
and they must never ever ever
be seen snogging each other in public
or anyone else for that matter

All children must eat the following
sweets
chocolate
pizza
chips
greasy burgers
bubble gum
crisps
all at the same time.

Paul Cookson and David Harmer

The Keystage Kids

They decided the sheriffs were useless
That the law was becoming a jest,
So the kids held a meeting in Keystage
And decided to clean up the West.

They pinned on the stars that their mums made,
Turned their very small horses about,
Hit the trail for the town known as Trouble:
The Keystage Kids boldly rode out.

At the head of the bunch is
Kent Westwood
With his trusty lieutenant
Wayne Johns;
Mitch Robbum is there
and Bob Bedford
And they all carry strange-
looking guns.

In Trouble, the trouble they're
seeking
Is the West's leanest, meanest outlaw
Who rides with a wild gang of hoodlums
And his name is Mad Morgan McGraw.

McGraw and his mob were all drinking
And cheating at cards. It was noon
When the Keystage Kids all hit the township
And burst into its noisy saloon.

Mad Morgan's mob went for their guns
But the K-Kids had got it all sussed:
They triggered their pepper pistols
And filled the saloon with their dust.

While the villains were choking and spluttering
The Kids' second wave made a catch:
Flung a tennis net over the outlaws.
To the Kids it was a game, set and match.

The McGraw mob was hurled in the hoosegow,
All handcuffed and tightly bound,
While the locals rejoiced and treated the Kids
To pop, crisps and peanuts all round.

And that's only the start of the legend
Of the kids who cleaned up the West.
If you should find yourself with a few hours to spare
Come back and I'll tell you the rest.

Eric Finney

from Lilliput Levee

Oh, what a wonderful change to see!
Nothing is dull as it used to be,
Since the children, by clever bold strokes,
Have turned the tables upon the old folks.

They seized the keys, patrolled the street,
Drove the policeman off his beat,
Built barricades and stationed sentries:
Give the word when you come to the entries!

They dressed themselves in rifleman's clothes;
They had pea-shooters and arrows and bows,
So as to put resistance down:
Order reigns in Lilliput Town.

They sucked the jam, they lost the spoons,
They sent up dozens of fire balloons,
They let off crackers, they burnt a guy,
They piled a bonfire ever so high.

They offered a prize for the laziest boy,
And one for the most magnificent toy;
They split or burnt the canes offhand,
And made new laws in Lilliput Land:

Never do today what you can
Put off till tomorrow, one of them ran;
Late to bed and late to rise,
Was another law which they devised.

Nail up the door, slide down the stairs,
Saw off the legs of the parlour chairs –
That was the way in Lilliput Land,
The children having the upper hand.

They made the old folks come to school
All in pinafores – that was the rule –
Saying *Eener-deener-diner-duss*,
Kattler-wheeler-whiler-wuss.

Now, since little folk wear the crown,
Order reigns in Lilliput Town;
And Jack is king and Jill is queen
In the very best government ever seen.

William Brightly Rands

My Daughter's the Head of the Fashion Police

My daughter's
The Head of the
Fashion Police round here.

She's worked at it.
She's met secretly
In dark corners
With her friends.
They've talked it through,
They've decided.

She's been to see me –
Presented their terms,
The bottom line.
She's given me –

The printout

The details
Are all there –
What I
Must not ever
Be seen in
(At any time)
Out of doors
Especially when

It is possible that
One of her friends
Might see me.

I shall not wear
Cardigans
Or sailor caps
Or slacks
Or lime-green fleeces
Or checked shirts
Or psychedelic ties
Or tartan jackets
Or slip-on shoes
Or pop flares
(at my age)
Or turquoise suits.

And in particular –
Anything
That's beige.

Additionally,
I shall not wear
Tennis shoes
Or cravats.

I shall replace my new
Reading glasses
Which
(Apparently)
Make me look like an owl.

I undertake
Never to
Wear purple braces
And I shall give
All of
My Hawaiian shirts
To the poor
And the needy
(By tomorrow morning
At the very latest)

I shall
Try to be

I *must*
Try to be

Er . . .

How did she describe it . . . ?

Ah yes –
Cool . . .   *John Turner*

If I Ruled the World

If I ruled the world
I'd draw disharmony to an end.

There'd be no more painful
love triangles

or degrees of
unhelpful compromise.

There'd be no more pointless,
circular conflicts –

no more squaring up
of unequal sides.

If I ruled the world
I'd put everything straight.

Philip Waddell

The Klorine Kid

They call me the Klorine Kid,
I go swimming every day.
They call me the Klorine Kid,
I'm the King of the Baths, OK?

Make a splash
Make waves
Belly up
Not afraid
Roll over
Belly down
Never scared
Of going down

Deep end
Shallow end
Catch my breath
Not the bends
Try a dive
From the top
Watch out for
The belly flop

Pupil Power

Call me if you need a leader
I'm so cool. I'm no fool.
I could easily rule this school.

Tell the head he must resign.
With me instead, we'll all do fine,
Trust me cos I'm nearly nine.
Beneath each desk'll be a den
Out-of-bounds if you're over ten.

I'm so cool. I'm no fool.
I could easily rule this school.

Make me the resident Primary president,
Prince of the playground, king of the classroom
Private apartment in the staffroom.

I'm so cool. I'm no fool.
I could easily rule this school.

Any pupil who sits still
Will be sent home cos they're ill.
Break'll be from ten till three,
With Cartoon Network on TV,
Cans of cherryade given out free,
Chips and chewing gum on demand.
Lessons and learning will be banned.

I'm so cool. I'm no fool.
I could easily rule this school.

Dinner in school will be a treat.
Bin your veg and bin your meat.
Have a whole heap of sickly sweet
Stuff you're told you shouldn't eat.

I'm so cool. I'm no fool.
I could easily rule this school.

Elect me now or be too late.
Kids from elsewhere think I'm great.
I'm so cool. I'm no fool.
They'll pay me to rule their school.

Nick Toczek

Matthew (Aged 9) is the Referee

Ha ha ha, tee hee hee
I am the ref and the ref is me
I am Matthew, I'm in charge
not very tall, not very large
don't you worry you will see
I'm a brilliant referee
so kids v teachers, off we go
wait to hear my whistle blow.

Offside there Mr Leek
for those awful sums last week
a yellow card Mrs Best
for that rotten spelling test

that's handball Mr Poole
you kept me in after school
a terrible tackle by Miss Clark
my story got a very low mark
and as for you Mr Lime
who kept me in all dinnertime
for hearing something that I said
sorry pal, this card is red.
What was that Mrs Cook?
Don't shoot me that filthy look
you and Mrs Jones are off
And Mr Yates and Mrs Gough
with your goalie Mr Slack
for elbowing my mate Jack.

OK kids, most of the staff
are off the field in the early
bath
with any luck you will score
about a million goals or more
take it steady, cool and slow
there's still the second half to go.

Ha ha ha, tee hee hee
I am the ref and the ref is me
I am Matthew, I'm in charge

David Harmer

Dear Mrs James

Dear Mrs James,
I've decided to keep mum at home today.
School and everything's getting her down,
she's got parent burnout, it's all got too much,
what with as well as takeing me and Ed

and Danny and Jane next door in every day
and bringing us home, Tuesdays
she collects me after my guitarrh lesson
and waits while Danny has maths coatching
round Mr Fellows' house then Wedensdays
is my football practise plus a lift
to evening rehersals for Ed for Cats
in the village hall. Thursdays after school
is extra tests for Sats for me, and Fridays
before school it's speling club which dad says
I have to go to I don't see why. Saturday morning
their's football a match and Saturday afternoon
we go family shopping. So I rung up the docter
and asked can she give mum some rest pills
or something but she says to take her out to lunch
on the bus with money from dad and go shopping
for clothes or something and get some flowers
and keep her away from the car which is what
we're doing. So I'm not coming to school today
or tomorrow probably because this is inportant
I know youll agree and be simperthetic,
take care, see you Monday, love, Melissa.

Robert Hull

Twenty-Two Things You Are Now Allowed to Do in Tests

Make rude faces at the teachers
Shout out loud and wave
   'Yoo-hoo!'
Flick elastic bands
Sneeze on the kid in front of you

Eat a bag of onion crisps
Whistle a happy tune
Blow your nose like a trombone
Somersault around the room

Stick a pencil up your nose
Lean back on your seat
Make those armpit trumpet sounds
Be sick on your answer sheet

Pretend you are a wasp
Fiddle with your underwear
Take your sweaty trainers off
Hiccup six feet in the air

Clap the answers in Morse Code
Bounce your rubber on the floor
Twang tunes with your ruler
Have beans for tea the night before

Daydream, snooze and slowly snore
Burp loudly halfway through
If you have to do a test . . .
Twenty-two things that you can do!

Paul Cookson

A Life of Adventure

My bed
is a spaceship.

My pyjamas
are my spacesuit.

My bedroom is outer space.

When the light goes out
We have lift-off.

I hurtle towards planet sleep
and explore that world
until it is time to leave.

At first light
We have touchdown.

A safe landing.

I rise from my spaceship.
Rinse off the space dust.
Put on my earth clothes
and report to Mission Control.

I eat breakfast
and board the bus for school.

The school bus
is a submarine.

My school uniform
is a submarine commander's uniform.

The road I travel on
becomes the ocean I dive to the bottom of.

Bernard Young

Swapping Spell

Windswept cliff and creepy cave,
Make my uncle be my slave!
Make him serve me, meek and grave,
While I shout and rant and rave!

Spider black and cobra blue,
Make my aunt my servant too!
Make her serve me good and true,
While I tell her what to do!

Kate Williams

If I Was in Charge

I'd say
Sit down!
Be quiet!
Take out your reading books.
Read silently!

I'd then
Peruse
My *Beano*
And drink a cup
Of tea.

Roger Stevens

When I am the England Manager . . .

All opposition teams wear pink.
And play in fluffy teddy-bear slippers and tutus.

Their goalposts must be twenty-feet high
and thirty-five-feet wide
while ours can be reduced and moved
at a touch of a remote-controlled button
in my tracksuit pocket.

Matches will finish when I decide it is appropriate,
but only when we have scored more goals and are winning.
So games could last for three hours, a week, a month
or the full-time whistle may be blown
after two minutes if we get an early breakthrough.

Floodlights can be angled and altered in such a way
so that opposing goalkeepers are dazzled on high crosses.
Should that not work they can then be switched on and off
continuously until the desired effect is achieved.

In hot and humid matches
we are allowed to wear as much suntan cream as we want,
drink as much water and isotonic fluid as we want
and have a rest whenever we want.
The opposition however
can only use cooking oil and *Deep Heat*
and must drink salt water and hot curried vegetable soup.

In cold and freezing conditions
we will wear our woolly gloves and hats,
thermal underwear and centrally heated shorts
but they must play in their pants and vests.
Or skins.

When we have a free kick
defensive walls *can* stand within ten yards
although players are *not* allowed
to protect themselves with their hands.

We must receive at least one penalty per game
while opposing goalkeepers are only allowed oven gloves
and a pair of horse's blinkers.

Our goalies meanwhile
can utilize radar to detect dangerous crosses
and the liberal application of superglue.

World Cups will be ours,
the European Championships will be a formality
and record books will be rewritten forever
when I am the England Manager.

Paul Cookson

Wishing on a Star

Well, now I'm a policeman.
I wished on a star
and now I'm a policeman
in a police car
I've arrested my teacher,
our caretaker too
along with a horrible
bully called Sue.
I've arrested an aunt
and my dentist as well
and I'm putting them,
all of them, into a cell
and there I shall leave them,
on water and bread
while I make one more journey
to bring in the Head.
Yes, now I'm a policeman,
I think they will see
that they all should have been
much, much nicer to me.

Marian Swinger

It's Hard but I'll Manage!

It's funny, but since becoming Prime Minister my parents
Don't seem to boss me around
As much any more!

(Still it must be hard to boss anyone around when you're
Gagged and tied up in the attic!)

And since becoming Prime Minister my sister doesn't
Seem to annoy me with her loud music
Half as much as she did!

(But then again it must be hard to put your stereo on in
the first place when there's a
Snarling Rottweiler chained to it!)

And since becoming Prime Minister I've noticed
That my older brother has completely
Given up bullying me!

(Hardly surprising though, regular electric shocks
Would change most people's attitude!)

Yes, things have certainly changed since I became
The Prime Minister on my tenth birthday last week,

Change is hard, but I'm sure I'll get used to it!

Ian Bland

Mother! Things Must Change Around Here

Untidy your bedroom.
It's looking far too neat.
And, unless you answer back,
I'll put you in the street.

Throw your coat down in the hall.
Don't hang it on a peg.
Burst open several bags of crisps
and devour them like a pig.

I hope you're not intending
to wash behind your ears.
If I find your neck's not dirty
there will be some tears.

And at every opportunity
you must watch TV.
I shall be very annoyed
if you're not glued to the set like me.

As for cooking, cleaning, laundry
– those jobs are still to do.
So cooking, cleaning, laundry
– those chores belong to you.

And, last but not least,
the most important new rule –
I shall be staying home.
You will be going to school.

Bernard Young

A Spell in Office

When I am Prime Minister
I'll make warlocks welcome
and witches persona much grata,
with covens encouraged to multiply.

I'll set up workshops for making broomsticks,
degree courses in cloak and pointy hat design,
and breeding programmes for owls and black cats.
I'll build mega-stores with special departments:
Dark Arts for books and magazines with the latest spells,
Cookware for cauldrons,
a deadlycatessan for yukky ingredients,
Per Zoomer for warm underwear for night flights –
all under one roof with an invisible landing pad
and two hours' free parking.

I'll decree a Hallowe'en at each month's end
with no All Saints' Day after,
outlaw witchist comments,
make discrimination a bed spell offence.

And, when I'm Prime Minister,
I'll be able to do all this
without even being . . . scared.

Hilary Tinsley

Kids Rule OK

When Kids rule, Kids rule
From London Town to Liverpool,
When Kids rule the whole UK
When kids rule – when it's our day
When kids rule the world – OK,
Then we won't care what grown-ups say.

When Kids rule, Kids rule
From Amsterdam to Istanbul,
We'll tell the teachers what to do,
Send all parents to Timbuktu –
Make older sisters go there too
And everyone who's well to do.
When Kids rule the whole UK
When kids rule – when it's our day
When kids rule the world – OK.

With Kid-power, you'll agree –
The Kids will have the master key,
With Kid-power, you will see
We'll have a Kids' democracy.

When Kids rule, Kids rule,
There'll be no more school –
And we'll spend all day
Looking very cool,
Sitting in our shades
At the swimming pool.

When Kids rule, kids rule,
Holidays will last all year –
Tons of free designer gear,
The taps will run with cool root beer
And know-it-alls who interfere
Will all be made to disappear,
When Kids rule the whole UK
When kids rule – when it's our day
When kids rule the world – OK.

Annoying dads with annoying jokes,
Annoying aunts who pinch and poke,
Annoying mums who say they're broke –
They'll all go up in a puff of smoke,
When Kids rule the whole UK
When kids rule – when it's our day
When kids rule the world – **OK**.

John Turner

Decision Time

'ORDER! ORDER!
The Speaker cried.

'We'll have burgers and chips,'
The MPs replied.

Trevor Harvey

King Pong

Now I'm crowned I don't wash my feet,
wear clean socks or keep my room neat.
My mum whispers, 'Sire,
have you changed your attire?'
Cos I've worn the same undies all week.

Celia Gentles

Fit for a King

Sausages for breakfast,
For dinner and for tea:
When I am King of England,
More sausages for me!

Sausages with bacon,
Tomatoes, eggs, fried bread:
When I am King of England
I mean to be well fed.

Sausages and mushrooms,
Black pudding and brown sauce:
When I am King of England,
Baked beans as well, of course.

Sausages and hash-browns –
Then toast and jam and tea:
When I am King of England,
What a chubby chap I'll be!

John Kitching

Small Changes in Government

Since taking over the running of the country we've:
replaced the Cabinet with one that holds
pop and crisps,
painted the door of Number Ten bright orange
(Black Rod is also in the same colour!)
and had skateboard ramps built in Downing Street –
to keep the wheels of Government turning!

We've replaced Prime Minister's Question Time
With a Car Boot Sale and Games Fayre.
(Now we have cash for items not questions!)

The House of Lords has also been modernised
The Wool Sack's been replaced with a
large beanbag
and a roller coaster is now installed in the Upper House –
to put the fun back into politics!

Instead of the State Opening of Parliament
we're having a disco with karaoke –
so all us MPs can sing our own praises!

To pay for all these changes,
we've introduced an Adult Chocolate Tax
which also helps the State subsidize
the rise
in children's pocket money!

Chris Ogden

The Anarchist

If they made me Head teacher for the day
My first law would be really clever
I'd lock all the teachers in the lav
And make playtime last forever.

Gareth Owen

The Minister of Awe and Wonder

To watch the sun rise every morn,
To hear the sounds of breaking dawn.
To marvel at new buds that grow
Through frosted ground and soil below.
To catch the first drop of rain in May
To stop and ponder every day.
To celebrate each storm and thunder
For I am the Minister of Awe and Wonder.

To view the gold of Autumn leaves
To speculate how rivers freeze.
To watch a spider spin its web
With filaments of silken thread.
To stare and gaze with fresh surprise
To view the world with child's eyes.
Admire, respect but never plunder
So says the Minister of Awe and Wonder.

Chris Ogden

The School Day

Introducing the five-minute school day
Which begins just after play
And ends just before lunch

If you are late
That's great
You'll have to try again tomorrow.

Unless the day has an 's' in it
Or comes after Sunday
Or immediately before Sunday

John Coldwell

Our School is Revolting

Me and my mate are taking charge
He'll be corporal, I'll be sarge.
Our pupil army will be large
And through the school we'll boldly barge.

And after we have taken charge
We'll phone for pizzas, extra-large,
And force the Head to foot the charge
But put the staff on bread-and-marge.

Nick Toczek

Mighty Ben

Ben lived down where the world is grey
And the kids hang round the streets all day.
You have to be tough to live round there
Cos life's like that and life's not fair.

Now Ben's old grandpa used to say
He was born in a place that's far away,
Where bananas grow and parrots fly
And the big yellow sun never leaves the sky.
'There's no such place as that!' says Ben.
'Old Gramp's been having his dream again!'

Then Grandpa laughs, 'You might be right
But when I'm rich I'll take that flight
Cos listen here, Ben, I'm telling you
There are no dreams that can't come true.'

Now Ben had a secret fantasy,
He thought how brilliant it would be
If he had powers to fly around
And clear up all the trouble in town,
And the bit of his dream he liked the best
Was the letters MB on his bright-red vest.

One rainy night as he lay in bed
He remembered what his gramp had said:
'Now listen here, Ben, I'm telling you
There are no dreams that can't come true.'

Then lightning flashed, and by its glare,
Ben saw something on his chair.
He reached the switch, turned on the lights
And found a golden cloak, green tights,
A pair of boots, and finally,
A bright-red vest, with a big MB.

Ben didn't hang around to think,
He put on those things as quick as a blink.
With superpowers it wouldn't take long
To hit the town and right some wrongs.

His toughest foe was a guy called Joss,
He had a gang and he was boss
And the worst of all the things he did
Was to sell bad stuff to little kids.
Ben swept the town with X-ray eyes
To find the lair of those evil guys.

The lookout man cried, 'Aaagh!' and then,
'Is it a bird, or a plane? No, it's Mighty Ben!'
But Joss just laughed, said, 'What's the fuss?
He's only a kid, he can't stop us!'
He could – once Ben gets on your trail,
It's goodbye hope and hello jail.

So Ben flew home, a job done well,
What a tale he'd have to tell!
He threw his wet cloak on his chair –
When he woke next day it wasn't there.

It seemed so real; but now he knew
That Gramps was wrong, dreams can't come true.

Then underneath his chair he saw
A puddle of water on the floor . . .

David Orme

Since Sprouts Became Illegal, Sprout Smuggling has Become a Huge Problem

Attention!
Be on your guard
Be vigilant – alert.
They are everywhere
The sprout smugglers
Carrying their green disgusting cargo.

Look carefully at those old ladies
And don't be fooled
By rosy-apple smiles
And cosy cardigans.

Note the strange lumpiness
Of their stockings
Ask yourself just what's inside
Those pink hand-knitted teddy bears . . . ?

Last week we caught a gang of sprouters
With sack loads of the stuff
Grown secretly on clandestine allotments
And then concealed
Inside consignments of red Santa suits.
They're cunning. Ruthless.

So be watchful.
Remember
It's December
And throughout the land
There are turkey dinners planned.
Carrots we can cope with,
But your job, without a doubt,
Is to save the nation's children
From the horror
Of the Christmas dinner sprout.

Jan Dean

Just What the Doctor Ordered

You've got a sore throat?
Then take six weeks off.
You can't go to school
with that terrible cough.
I prescribe somewhere warm
so pop down the corridor
and collect a prescription
for Disneyland, Florida.
Next, please. A sprained ankle?
I advise many toys
which speed the recovery
of girls and of boys.
Make them expensive,
We don't need a subscription.
I'll just write you out
a nice, big, prescription.
Any more patients?
Ah yes, Annabel.
And what can I do for you?
You don't look too well.

Your teacher is nasty!
Called you a dunce!
Then I prescribe you
a year off at once
to be taken in Spain
on a hot, golden beach
to refresh all those parts
which school cannot reach.
Next please. Ah, wee Georgie.
No appetite?
A prescription of sweeties

will soon put that right
and here's pretty Petunia.
You're increasing in size?
I'll prescribe you a puppy.
The brisk exercise
you get taking a puppy
out for a run
is invigorating,
healthful and fun.
Well, that's my last patient.
It's been a good day
and your doctor (aged nine)
is now off out to play.

Marian Swinger

If I were in Charge

If I were the master of contagious diseases,
And made the decisions on who would be ill,
I'd make sure the bullies went down with the sneezes
And big brothers would shrink after popping a pill.

If I were an expert at treating infections
And was able to cure the nastiest spots,
I'd use a pea-shooter for giving injections
And aim for the targets I'd pinned to their bots!

If I were an amazing medicine mixer
I'd mix a concoction that tasted of wine.
I'd make sure the teachers drank up the elixir
which would send them to sleep for a very long time!

If I were a professor of peculiar potions
I'd make one, that made people have a good time
Their hearts would be full, of love and devotion
They wouldn't have time for fighting and crime!

If I were the king of itches and scratches
I'd give all the MPs a dose of the nits.
They'd be so busy scratching bald patches
That the country would all fall to bits!

Diane Humphrey

If I were the Leader

If I were the duke
Of oh-what-a-fluke
Then life would be a ball.

If I were the head
Of lying-in-bed
I'd never get up at all.

If I were in charge
Of everyone large
I wouldn't be pushed about.

If I were the boss
Of ever-so-cross
I'd stamp and scream and shout.

If I were the prince
Of only-a-rinse
There'd be no showers or baths.

If I were the lord
Of never-be-bored
We'd have no rain or maths.

If I were the chief
Of bacon-and-beef
I'd eat whatever I chose.

If I were the king
Of everything
I'd really get up your nose.

Nick Toczek

Now Children Rule

Children of the world,
now that we rule, we will be as one nation.

Children of the starved lands
now that we rule, we will feed you.

Mad dictators and makers of war,
now that we rule, your voices shall be ignored
and you will dwindle into nothingness . . .

Deluded priests and fanatical fools,
now that we rule, we will laugh at you
and your churches and temples will fall into dust.

Weapons of destruction,
now that we rule, you yourselves will be destroyed.

Cousins in fur and feather,
now that we rule, we shall leave space for you too.

Mighty oceans,
now that we rule, no poisons will be poured into your
    vast deeps.

Wild wind,
now that we rule, no evil fumes will sully your purity.

Flowers of the field,
now that we rule, you shall pour your sweetness into the
    spring air.

Great trees of the steaming jungle,
now that we rule, your green canopy will spread to
    protect the world.

Grown-ups,
now that we rule, you will behave yourselves.

Marian Swinger

A Minor Glitch
(as explained by the PM's Personal Private Secretary)

The Prime Minister is not at home.
He's on his way back from Casualty
(nothing too serious)
after a nasty tumble
from his mountain bike.

The Prime Minister is not available.
He's reading a comic
and recuperating
in the ministerial
four-poster bed.

The Prime Minister is unable to comment.
Unfortunately
he's banged his jaw,
bitten his tongue
and can't utter a word.

*The Prime Minister will not be attending Parliament
for the next two or three days.*
He'll he far too busy
touring the shops
in the official Daimler
and choosing a new bike.

Patricia Leighton

Small Change

I'm two years old, can't read or write,
Of savings, I've not any;
I've just been made the 'Chancellor' –
That's why I've spent a penny!

The thought of all those piles of coins
Has made me very happy!
I'm so EXCITED at the news –
Can someone change my nappy . . . ?

Trevor Harvey

Being 10 Years Old and the
Prime Minister Isn't Easy

They whined when I stuck chewing gum
Under the table during my audience with the Queen

They griped when I skateboarded down the stairs
At 10 Downing Street

They whinged when I had my Walkman on during
Prime Minister's Question Time

But when I giggled and screamed and bellowed and wailed
Like an animal in The Houses of Parliament

I fitted in quite nicely

Ian Bland

The Junior Head Teacher Addresses
a Staff Meeting

After a number of complaints from children
I have to remind you
Yet again
About
Staff school uniform
Shirts must not be tucked in
Top buttons must be undone at all times
Ties must be knotted just above the waist
Blazers should be screwed up and placed in the
    bottom of bags
Shoelaces should not be tied.

I have also been told that some teachers are
Arriving at lessons on time
And
Setting homework.
This must stop at once

Lastly,
Will you please remember
That the lunch hour
Is seventy minutes long

John Coldwell

Power

Yes, here I am.
your teacher for the day,
your very own classmate.
But don't think I'll let you off work.
Oh no!
You will work twice as hard for me.
Three times as hard.
All those who have bullied me
in the last six months,
come to the front.
Good.
Now I'll make you suffer.
First, a maths test
which I know you will all fail.
Any questions?
Good.
Settle down.
Anyone who talks, chews, fidgets,
or picks their nose gets detention.
Ah, this is wonderful.
When I grow up I shall be a dictator.
A world dictator!
Ha ha.

Ow! Unhand me Miss Pomfret
or I shall tell my mother of your brutality.
Yes. I was paying attention.
No. I was not daydreaming in class.
I heard every word you said.

Marian Swinger

The Hero

The Captain's collapsed. Don't panic, folks,
I'll fly the plane. It's not a joke.
Yes, I know I'm just a child
but fasten seatbelts, don't go wild.
Calm down stewardesses, please.
I can land this crate with ease.
Just let me have the Captain's chair.
You can drag him over there.
I'll bring her in to land, don't scream.
This may only be a dream
but while it lasts, I am (touch wood)
flying high and feeling good.

Marian Swinger

If I Ruled the World . . .

I would control the weather.
It would always rain on my big brother,
sometimes big plopping drops
just as he's about to go out to his mate's
and he'd not know whether to be cool without a coat
and get soaked, or look daft in a cagoule.

Then when he's on his bike
I'd make sure it was boiling hot as he set off
then it would drizzle that really wetting rain
so he'd look stupid in sunglasses and they'd steam up
and by the time he got home
he'd be freezing to the bones.

My brother would never be invited to picnics
or theme parks, or any outdoor event
because he would always bring the rain with him
and people couldn't understand it
but they'd still never invite him all the same.

If I controlled the weather
I would make sure it never rained
on me on Saturday afternoons,
and then I wouldn't have to stay in
playing boring games
with my Dad saying 'come on concentrate
it's your turn, at this rate you'll never win.'

Perhaps it's just as well
I don't control the weather
I'd make the sun shine every day
And stay at the beach forever!

Lesley Marshall

Teachers' Playtime

It's wonderful being on duty
When the teachers come out to play
See them running and shouting and leaping about
On a sunny winter's day

But I have sent Mr Walton
Back to the class for his coat
And Miss Wimple's stayed in – there's a spot on her chin
(Her mother sent a note)

Ms Bludgeon hits Mr Owen
She says he has stolen her ball
So I give her a lecture about sharing and caring
And I make her stand in the hall

Mrs Winger falls over and twists her foot
She's limping, but there's nothing to see
So I ask her to zoom to the staffroom
To fetch me my cup of tea

Mrs Prior's chasing Mr Owen
He's hiding in the boys' bog
He says he'll stay there all day if she won't go away
Cos she's trying to give him a snog

Mrs Lopez, who works in the office,
Does a handstand against the wall
You can see her navy-blue knickers.
It's not very nice at all.

I love it on playground duty.
Bossing teachers still gives me a thrill.
So I ring the bell two minutes early.
And . . .

Mr Walton . . .

STAND STILL!

Roger Stevens

If Children Ruled the World

If children ruled the world
vegetables would be banned
and adults sent to bed at eight
right across the land.

Teachers would wear uniform
and be told what to do,
they'd have to sit in rows all day
with no trips to the loo.

Weekends would be sunny
school dinners would taste great,
grannies wouldn't try to kiss
and parents wouldn't be late.

Things would be much better
if only for a day,
so let's give children a chance
to do things just their way.

Andrew Collett

My Cabinet

The Minister of Agriculture
brings lambs to the meeting.

The Minister for Food and Fish
is nearly always eating.

The Minister for Transport
leaves his skateboard by the door.

The Minister for Science
asks what everything is for.

The Minister of Art
is going to decorate my office.

The Minister for Health
always asks me how my cough is.

The Minister of Literature
is writing me a poem.

The Chancellor of the Exchequer
wants two pounds I owe him.

The Minister for Music
comes in whistling merrily.

And then there is the one
with lots of great ideas – me.

I've got a very clever team
in my Cabinet

despite the small amount
of pocket money that we get.

Jill Townsend

The Missing Headmaster

Where has our young headmaster gone?
Whatever is he at?
The chairman of the governors
is waiting for a chat.
We've searched throughout the dinner-break.
We've hunted far and wide.
He isn't in the building,
so he must have gone outside.

Is that his giggle on the wind?
What are those cracking sounds?
We thought that corner of the field
was strictly out of bounds.
Whatever is he doing there
beneath the chestnut trees?
Good gracious!
Who'd believe it?
Playing conkers, if you please!

Barry Buckingham

Batman

Batman
Age 10½
Patrols the streets of his suburb
At night
Between 7 and 8 o'clock.
If he is out later than this
he is spanked
and sent to bed
Without supper.

Batman
Almost 11
Patrols the streets of his suburb
At night
If he has finished his homework.

Batman,
His secret identity
And freckles
Protected
By the mask and cloak
His Auntie Elsie
Made on her sewing machine,
Patrols
At night
Righting Wrongs.

Tonight he is on the trail of
Raymond age 11
(large for his age)
Who has stolen Stephen's
Gobstoppers and football cards.

Batman
Patrolling the streets of his suburb
Righting Wrongs
Finds Raymond
Demands the return of stolen goods.
Raymond knocks him over,
Rips his mask,
Tears his cloak,
And steals his utility belt.

Batman starts to cry,
Wipes his eyes with his cape
(His hankie was in the belt).

Next day
Auntie Elsie says
This is the fourteenth time
I've had to mend your
Batman costume.
If it happens again
You'll have to whistle for it.

Batman
Eats a bag of crisps.

John Turner